XKHORT COMEDY

THE BUSINESS

Contents

1 BUSINESS — 1

2 BUSINESS ANALYTICS — 4

3 START UP IDEAS — 9

4 Eco-Friendly Products — 12

5 Online Education — 15

6 Virtual Events and Experiences — 18

7 Health and wellness services — 21

8 Mobile App Development — 25

9 Subscription Boxes — 29

10 Home Renovation and Design — 34

11 Pet Services — 39

12 Digital Marketing Agency — 44

13 Elderly Care and Assistance — 49

14 Conclusion — 54

One

BUSINESS

Business refers to the organized efforts, activities, and interactions undertaken by individuals or organizations to produce, sell, or trade goods and services with the goal of generating profit. It involves various aspects such as planning, production, marketing, sales, finance, and management. Businesses can take many forms, including sole proprietor-ships, partnerships, corporations, and more. They play a crucial role in the economy by creating jobs, driving innovation, and contributing to the overall growth and development of societies.

Certainly! Business is a complex and multifaceted concept. It encompasses a wide range of activities and functions, including:

1. **Entrepreneurship**: The process of identifying opportunities, taking risks, and creating new ventures or products.
2. **Management**: The practice of coordinating resources,

people, and processes to achieve the goals of the business.

3. **Marketing**: The activities aimed at promoting and selling products or services to customers, including market research, advertising, and branding.

4. **Finance**: Managing the financial aspects of a business, including budgeting, investing, and tracking financial performance.

5. **Operations**: The day-to-day processes and activities that produce goods or deliver services, ensuring efficiency and quality.

6. **Human Resources**: Handling recruitment, training, and management of employees, as well as addressing workplace issues.

7. **Supply Chain**: Managing the flow of goods and services from suppliers to customers, including procurement, logistics, and distribution.

8. **Innovation**: Developing new ideas, products, or processes that can give a business a competitive edge.

9. **Economics**: Business activities have a significant impact on local, national, and global economies, influencing factors like employment rates, GDP, and trade.

10. **Corporate Social Responsibility (CTR)**: Many businesses focus on ethical and sustainable practices, giving back to the community and minimizing negative impacts on the environment.

11. **Globalization**: With advancements in technology and communication, businesses now operate on a global scale, impacting international trade and cultural exchange.

12. **Risk Management**: Identifying potential risks and implementing strategies to mitigate them, ensuring the stability and continuity of the business.

Businesses can vary in size, scope, and industry. They can be small local shops, multinational corporations, online startups, service providers, manufacturers, and more. The world of business is dynamic, constantly evolving in response to changing markets, technology, consumer preferences, and regulatory environments

Two

BUSINESS ANALYTICS

Business analytics refers to the practice of using data analysis and statistical methods to gain insights, make informed decisions, and improve overall business performance. It involves collecting, processing, and analyzing data from various sources within a business to identify patterns, trends, and correlations that can inform strategic and operational decisions.

Business analytics involves several key components:

1. **Data Collection**: Gathering data from various sources, such as customer transactions, website interactions, social media, and more.
2. **Data Processing**: Cleaning and organizing the collected data to ensure its accuracy and reliability.
3. **Data Analysis**: Applying various techniques, including statistical analysis, data mining, and predictive modeling,

to uncover meaningful insights from the data.

4. **Data Visualization**: Presenting the analyzed data in the form of charts, graphs, dashboards, and other visual representations to make it easier to understand and interpret.
5. **Descriptive Analytics**: Examining historical data to understand what has happened in the past and identify trends and patterns.
6. **Predictive Analytics**: Using historical data to make predictions about future outcomes and trends.
7. **Prescriptive Analytics**: Recommending actions or strategies based on the insights gained from data analysis.

Business analytics is used in various areas of business, including:

- **Marketing**: Analyzing customer behavior and preferences to create targeted marketing campaigns and optimize advertising strategies.
- **Operations**: Monitoring and optimizing supply chain, inventory, and production processes to improve efficiency.
- **Finance**: Analyzing financial data to make informed investment decisions, manage budgets, and identify cost-saving opportunities.
- **Customer Service**: Identifying areas for improvement in customer service by analyzing feedback and interaction data.
- **Risk Management**: Assessing potential risks and uncertainties using data analysis to make informed decisions on risk mitigation strategies.
- **Strategic Planning**: Using data-driven insights to shape business strategies and goals.

Business analytics plays a vital role in modern business management, helping organizations make evidence-based decisions, respond to market changes, and stay competitive in a rapidly evolving business landscape

Certainly, here are some more specific ideas and concepts related to business analytics:

1. **Big Data Analytics**: Dealing with large volumes of data to extract meaningful insights. This involves technologies like Hadoop and specialized tools for handling massive datasets.

2. **Machine Learning**: Using algorithms and statistical models to enable systems to learn from data and make predictions or decisions without being explicitly programmed.

3. **Customer Segmentation**: Dividing customers into distinct groups based on characteristics and behaviors, allowing businesses to tailor their marketing strategies.

4. **Churn Prediction**: Identifying customers who are likely to stop using a product or service, enabling proactive retention efforts.

5. **A/B Testing**: Comparing two versions of a web-page, email, or other content to determine which one performs better in terms of user engagement or conversion rates.

6. **Sentiment Analysis**: Assessing public sentiment from social media, reviews, and comments to understand customer opinions and reactions.

7. **Supply Chain Analytics**: Optimizing the supply chain process to ensure efficient inventory management, reduced lead times, and minimized costs.

8. **Fraud Detection**: Using data analysis to identify unusual

patterns or behaviors that could indicate fraudulent activities.

9. **Healthcare Analytics**: Analyzing patient data to improve healthcare outcomes, manage patient populations, and enhance operational efficiency.

10. **Retail Analytics**: Understanding buying patterns, foot traffic, and inventory turnover to make data-driven decisions about pricing, stock levels, and promotions.

11. **Financial Forecasting**: Using historical financial data to predict future financial performance and make informed investment decisions.

12. **Text Mining**: Extracting valuable insights from unstructured text data, such as customer reviews, emails, and social media posts.

13. **Geo-spatial Analytics**: Analyzing geographical data to make location-based decisions, such as site selection for new stores or identifying areas with high demand.

14. **Operational Analytics**: Monitoring real-time data to optimize ongoing operations, such as adjusting production schedules based on demand fluctuations.

15. **Web Analytics**: Tracking and analyzing website traffic and user behavior to improve user experience and conversion rates.

16. **HR Analytics**: Using data to optimize human resource processes, such as employee recruitment, performance assessment, and talent management.

17. **Energy Consumption Analytics**: Analyzing energy usage data to identify areas for energy efficiency improvements.

18. **Logistics Analytics**: Optimizing transportation and distribution processes for cost savings and timely deliveries.

19. **Time Series Analysis**: Analyzing data points collected over time to identify patterns and trends.
20. **Social Network Analysis**: Studying relationships within social networks to understand influence and connections.

These ideas demonstrate the diverse range of applications and benefits that business analytics can offer to different industries and aspects of business operations

Three

START UP IDEAS

Certainly, here are 10 business startup ideas across various industries:

1. **Eco-Friendly Products**: Launch a business that offers environmentally friendly and sustainable products, such as reusable household items, Eco-friendly packaging, or organic skincare products.

2. **Online Education**: Create an online platform that offers courses, workshops, or tutorials on a specific skill or subject, catering to a global audience.

3. **Virtual Events and Experiences**: Organize and host virtual events, workshops, or experiences, such as virtual fitness classes, online cooking workshops, or virtual travel tours.

4. **Health and Wellness Services**: Start a business

offering health and wellness services, such as personalized fitness training, nutrition coaching, or mental health counseling.

5. **Mobile App Development**: Develop a mobile app that addresses a specific problem or need, such as a task management app, language learning app, or productivity tool.

6. **Subscription Boxes**: Curate and deliver subscription boxes with niche products or experiences, such as gourmet snacks, self-care items, or craft supplies.

7. **Home Renovation and Design**: Offer interior design and home renovation services, focusing on creating functional and aesthetically pleasing spaces for clients.

8. **Pet Services**: Launch a business catering to pet owners by offering services such as pet grooming, dog walking, or pet sitting.

9. **Digital Marketing Agency**: Provide digital marketing services to small businesses looking to improve their online presence, social media engagement, and digital advertising efforts.

10. **Elderly Care and Assistance**: Start a business that provides in-home care, companionship, and assistance to elderly individuals who want to maintain their independence.

Remember that the success of a startup idea depends on factors like market demand, competition, your unique value proposition, and your ability to execute the idea effectively. Conduct thorough market research and develop a solid business plan before diving into any startup venture

Eco-Friendly Products

Certainly! The first startup idea, "Eco-Friendly Products," involves creating a business that offers products that are environmentally friendly and sustainable. This concept capitalizes on the growing consumer demand for products that have a lower impact on the environment and promote sustainable living. Here's a more detailed explanation:

Idea: Eco-Friendly Products Startup

Concept: This startup focuses on producing and selling products that are designed to minimize harm to the environment throughout their life cycle. These products are often made from renewable or recycled materials and are intended to be reusable, biodegradable, or easily recyclable.

Examples of Products:

• Reusable water bottles and travel mugs to reduce single-use plastic waste.

- Biodegradable and compost-able household cleaning products.
- Eco-friendly clothing made from organic or sustainable materials.
- Bamboo or metal straws to replace plastic straws.
- Zero-waste personal care products like shampoo bars and reusable cotton pads.

Benefits:

- **Environmental Impact**: By offering Eco-friendly alternatives, the business contributes to reducing pollution, resource depletion, and plastic waste.
- **Consumer Demand**: Many consumers are actively seeking products that align with their environmental values, creating a growing market.
- **Brand Value**: Businesses focused on sustainability often build strong brand loyalty among Eco-conscious consumers.
- **Innovation**: The startup can explore creative and innovative ways to make products that are both functional and environmentally friendly.

Challenges:

- **Sourcing Materials**: Finding sustainable materials and suppliers that meet quality standards can be a challenge.
- **Educating Consumers**: Some consumers might not be fully aware of the benefits of Eco-friendly products, so educating them about these benefits is important.

- **Competition**: The market for Eco-friendly products is becoming more competitive, requiring unique selling points to stand out.

Marketing Strategy:

- Highlight the environmental benefits of the products through branding and marketing materials.
- Use social media platforms to showcase the products, share educational content, and engage with the Eco-conscious community.
- Collaborate with influences or environmental organizations to increase brand visibility.

Sustainability Focus: Consider implementing Eco-friendly practices in all aspects of the business, from packaging materials to production processes.

Starting an Eco-friendly products business not only addresses a significant market demand but also contributes positively to the planet. It's important to research consumer preferences, understand production logistics, and establish a strong brand that resonates with environmentally conscious consumers

Five

Online Education

Certainly! The second startup idea, "Online Education," involves creating an online platform that offers courses, workshops, or tutorials on a specific skill or subject. This concept leverages the power of the internet to provide accessible and valuable educational content to a global audience. Here's a more detailed explanation:

Idea: Online Education Startup

Concept: This startup focuses on providing educational content online, making it accessible to anyone with an internet connection. The content can range from academic subjects to practical skills, creative arts, professional development, and more.

Examples of Offerings:

- Language learning courses.
- Coding and programming tutorials.

- Cooking and baking classes.
- Art and music lessons.
- Business and entrepreneurship workshops.
- Fitness and yoga training.
- Test preparation courses.

Benefits:

- **Global Reach**: The online platform allows you to reach learners from around the world, breaking down geographical barriers.
- **Flexible Learning**: Learners can access courses at their own pace and schedule, catering to different learning styles.
- **Diverse Revenue Streams**: You can generate income through course sales, subscriptions, premium content, and partnerships.
- **Expertise Sharing**: Experts and enthusiasts can share their knowledge and skills with a wide audience.

Challenges:

- **Competition**: The online education space is competitive, so it's important to find a unique angle or teaching approach.
- **Quality Control**: Ensuring high-quality content and engaging learning experiences is crucial for customer satisfaction.
- **Technical Infrastructure**: Building a user-friendly platform with good video quality and interactive features is essential.

Marketing Strategy:

- Offer free introductory courses to attract users and show-case the value of your content.
- Utilize social media, content marketing, and online advertising to promote courses.
- Gather testimonials and reviews from satisfied learners to build credibility.
- Collaborate with influences or experts in the field to endorse your courses.

Technology Considerations: Invest in a user-friendly website or app that offers features like video hosting, progress tracking, quizzes, and discussion forums.

Starting an online education startup requires careful curriculum planning, technical setup, and a commitment to providing valuable and engaging learning experiences. It's a dynamic field that can have a positive impact on learners' lives while offering a business opportunity for educators and content creators

Six

Virtual Events and Experiences

Certainly! The third startup idea, "Virtual Events and Experiences," involves creating an online platform or service that offers virtual events, workshops, or experiences to individuals or groups. This concept capitalizes on the increasing demand for online entertainment, learning, and social interactions. Here's a more detailed explanation:

Idea: Virtual Events and Experiences Startup

Concept: This startup focuses on curating and hosting virtual events, workshops, and experiences that participants can engage in from the comfort of their own homes. These virtual experiences can range from fitness classes and cooking workshops to live performances and guided tours.

Examples of Offerings:

- Virtual fitness classes, including yoga, HILT, and dance.
- Online cooking workshops led by professional chefs.

- Live virtual concerts, performances, or stand-up comedy shows.
- Guided virtual travel tours to explore destinations around the world.
- Art and craft workshops where participants create alongside an instructor.
- Online gaming tournaments and es-ports events.
- Personal development workshops on topics like mindfulness and communication skills.

Benefits:

- **Global Accessibility**: Participants from different parts of the world can join without the need for travel.
- **Flexibility**: Events can accommodate various time zones, allowing a broader audience to attend.
- **Diverse Audience**: Virtual experiences can cater to a wide range of interests and demographics.
- **Scalability**: With the right technology, virtual events can accommodate large audiences.
- **Lower Costs**: Virtual events often have lower overhead costs compared to in-person events.

Challenges:

- **Technical Requirements**: Ensuring a smooth and glitch-free virtual experience requires solid technical infrastructure.
- **Engagement**: Keeping participants engaged and creating interactive experiences is essential for success.
- **Monetization**: Finding the right pricing model that bal-

ances accessibility and revenue generation can be a challenge.

Marketing Strategy:

- Use social media and online advertising to reach potential participants.
- Collaborate with influences or experts relevant to the event's theme to attract attendees.
- Offer limited-time promotions or early bird discounts to encourage early sign-ups.
- Encourage participants to share their experiences on social media for word-of-mouth promotion.

Technology Considerations: Invest in a user-friendly platform that supports live streaming, interactive features (like chat and Q&A), and secure payment processing.

Starting a virtual events and experiences startup requires a mix of creativity, technical know-how, and strong marketing efforts. Providing unique and memorable virtual experiences can create a sense of community and connection, making it a promising venture in the rapidly evolving digital landscape

Seven

Health and wellness services

Certainly! The fourth startup idea, "Health and Wellness Services," involves creating a business that offers a range of health and wellness services to individuals looking to improve their overall well-being. This concept taps into the growing demand for personalized health solutions and self-care practices. Here's a more detailed explanation:

Idea: Health and Wellness Services Startup

Concept: This startup focuses on providing services that support individuals in achieving their health and wellness goals. These services can encompass physical fitness, nutrition, mental health, and holistic well-being.

Examples of Services:

- Personalized fitness training and workout plans.
- Nutrition coaching and meal planning.

- Mental health counseling and therapy sessions.
- Yoga and meditation classes.
- Wellness retreats and workshops.
- Stress management and relaxation techniques.

Benefits:

- **Personalization**: Tailoring services to individual needs and goals can result in more effective outcomes.
- **Holistic Approach**: Addressing physical, mental, and emotional well-being can lead to comprehensive improvements.
- **Growing Demand**: The increasing focus on health and self-care makes this industry promising.
- **Positive Impact**: Your business can contribute to improving people's quality of life and overall happiness.

Challenges:

- **Qualifications**: Depending on the services offered, you may need to have certified professionals on your team.
- **Competition**: The health and wellness industry can be competitive, so finding a unique selling point is crucial.
- **Building Trust**: Establishing credibility and trust with clients is essential for success.

Marketing Strategy:

- Highlight success stories and testimonials from clients who have benefited from your services.
- Share educational content on health and wellness topics

through blogs, videos, and social media.
- Collaborate with local fitness centers, spas, or wellness events to increase brand visibility.
- Offer trial sessions or workshops to give potential clients a taste of your services.

Technology Considerations: Depending on the services offered, you might need platforms for online scheduling, virtual consultations, or fitness tracking.

Starting a health and wellness services startup requires a deep understanding of various aspects of well-being and a genuine commitment to helping people lead healthier lives. Providing evidence-based services, building a supportive community, and continuously improving your offerings can set your business up for success in this thriving industry.

Here are five more business startup ideas to consider:

1. **Mobile App Development for Seniors**: Create user-friendly mobile apps designed specifically for seniors, addressing their unique needs, such as health monitoring, social engagement, and easy communication with family.
2. **Green Energy Solutions**: Start a business that focuses on providing renewable energy solutions, such as solar panel installation, energy-efficient appliances, and smart home energy management systems.
3. **Remote Work Support Services**: Offer services that help companies and individuals transition smoothly to remote work, including setting up virtual offices, providing tech support, and offering remote team-building activities.
4. **Local Food Delivery Service**: Create a platform that connects consumers with local farmers and producers,

offering a convenient way to order fresh, locally sourced produce and products directly to their doorstep.

5. **Elderly Care Tech Solutions**: Develop technology products that cater to the needs of the elderly, such as wearable devices for health monitoring, smart home systems for safety, and communication tools for staying connected with family.
6. **Sustainable Fashion Brand**: Launch a clothing brand that prioritizes sustainability, using Eco-friendly materials, ethical production processes, and transparent supply chains to create stylish and environmentally conscious fashion.

Remember, the success of a startup idea depends on factors such as market demand, competition, your passion and expertise, and your ability to execute the idea effectively. Thorough market research and a well-defined business plan are essential steps to take before embarking on any startup venture

Eight

Mobile App Development

Certainly! The fifth startup idea, "Mobile App Development for Seniors," involves creating user-friendly mobile applications specifically tailored to the needs and preferences of elderly individuals. This concept recognizes the growing use of technology among seniors and aims to provide them with tools that enhance their quality of life. Here's a more detailed explanation:

Idea: Mobile App Development for Seniors Startup

Concept: This startup focuses on developing mobile applications that cater to the unique requirements of seniors. The apps should be intuitive, user-friendly, and designed to address various aspects of their well-being, connectivity, and convenience.

Examples of App Types:

- **Health Monitoring**: Apps that help seniors track their

health metrics, remind them of medications, and connect with healthcare providers.

- **Social Engagement**: Apps that facilitate video calls, message sharing, and online social interactions with friends and family.
- **Brain Training**: Apps with games and exercises designed to promote cognitive health and memory improvement.
- **Emergency Assistance**: Apps that provide quick access to emergency services and alert designated contacts in case of emergencies.
- **Local Services**: Apps that connect seniors with local services like transportation, meal delivery, and home maintenance.

Benefits:

- **Improved Well-Being**: Apps can contribute to seniors' physical, mental, and emotional well-being, enabling them to stay connected and engaged.
- **Simplified Technology**: By creating user-friendly apps, the startup can bridge the technology gap for seniors who may be less familiar with digital devices.
- **Market Potential**: The aging population presents a growing market for tech solutions that cater to their needs.
- **Positive Impact**: Your startup can make a meaningful difference in the lives of seniors by enhancing their independence and connectivity.

Challenges:

- **Usability**: Ensuring that the apps are intuitive and easy to use for seniors is critical.

- **Accessibility**: Considering factors like font size, color contrast, and touch screen sensitivity to accommodate varying levels of physical ability.
- **Education**: Providing resources and support to help seniors learn how to use the apps effectively.

Marketing Strategy:

- Partner with senior centers, retirement communities, and healthcare providers to promote your apps.
- Offer workshops and tutorials to teach seniors how to use the apps and maximize their benefits.
- Leverage online platforms frequented by seniors and their caregivers to spread awareness.

Technology Considerations: Focus on creating apps with simple interfaces, large icons, and clear instructions. Consider incorporating voice commands and accessibility features to enhance usability.

Starting a mobile app development startup for seniors requires a deep understanding of their needs, preferences, and potential challenges with technology. By creating apps that genuinely enhance their lives and provide valuable solutions, your startup can have a positive impact on this demographic while tapping into a growing market

Absolutely! Here are five more business startup ideas for your consideration:

1. **Virtual Reality Experiences**: Create a business that offers immersive virtual reality experiences, such as virtual

tours, training simulations, or entertainment content for various industries.

2. **Eco-Tourism and Sustainable Travel**: Start a travel company that focuses on organizing Eco-friendly and sustainable travel experiences, promoting responsible tourism practices.

3. **Personalized Nutrition and Meal Planning**: Launch a service that provides personalized nutrition plans and meal delivery based on individuals' dietary preferences, health goals, and restrictions.

4. **Elderly Companionship Services**: Create a service that connects trained companions with elderly individuals, offering companionship, assistance with daily activities, and social engagement.

5. **Remote Healthcare Services**: Develop a platform that offers remote medical consultations, diagnostics, and prescription services, providing accessible healthcare solutions to patients from their homes.

Each of these startup ideas presents unique opportunities to tap into growing markets and make a positive impact on various industries and communities. As you explore these concepts, consider your passion, expertise, and the needs of your target audience to find the best fit for your entrepreneurial journey.

Nine

Subscription Boxes

Certainly! "Subscription Boxes" is a popular business model where customers subscribe to receive a curated selection of products delivered to their doorstep on a regular basis. This concept offers convenience, surprise, and personalization, making it a versatile option for various industries. Here's a more detailed explanation:

Concept: Subscription boxes involve offering a themed assortment of products delivered to customers at regular intervals, often monthly. The products can vary widely based on the niche or theme of the subscription box, such as beauty products, snacks, books, fitness gear, crafts, and more.

How It Works:

1. **Curated Selection**: The subscription box provider curates a selection of products based on a specific theme, interest, or niche. The products are often sourced from

various brands and suppliers.

2. **Subscription Plans**: Customers choose a subscription plan that suits their preferences and budget. Plans can range from monthly to quarterly and can be prepaid for a set duration.

3. **Personalization**: Some subscription boxes offer customization options where customers can indicate their preferences, sizes, or dietary restrictions to receive products tailored to their needs.

4. **Delivery**: The curated box is shipped to the customer's address at regular intervals, such as once a month or once every few months.

5. **Unboxing Experience**: Customers receive the box and experience the excitement of unboxing and discovering the products inside.

6. **Recurring Billing**: Customers are billed automatically according to their chosen subscription plan.

Benefits:

- **Convenience**: Customers receive a variety of products without the need to shop individually.
- **Discovery**: Subscription boxes introduce customers to new products and brands they might not have encountered otherwise.
- **Personalization**: Some boxes allow customers to personalize their selections, creating a more tailored experience.
- **Surprise and Delight**: The surprise element of unboxing adds excitement and anticipation to the experience.
- **Loyalty**: Subscribers often develop a sense of loyalty and connection with the brand providing the subscription.

Challenges:

- **Product Curation**: Selecting products that consistently meet customer expectations and preferences can be challenging.
- **Logistics and Fulfillment**: Managing inventory, packing, and shipping logistics efficiently is essential for a seamless experience.
- **Customer Retention**: Keeping subscribers engaged and satisfied to ensure they continue their subscriptions over time.

Marketing Strategy:

- Clearly communicate the unique value and theme of the subscription box.
- Use social media and influences to generate buzz and showcase unboxing experiences.
- Offer special promotions and discounts for new subscribers.

Subscription boxes can cater to a wide range of interests, making them a versatile business model that can be adapted to various niches. Whether it's beauty, wellness, food, books, or hobbies, subscription boxes offer a convenient and engaging way for customers to receive curated products regularly.

Certainly! Here are some additional aspects to consider when starting a subscription box business:

Niche Selection: Choose a specific niche or theme for your subscription box that resonates with your target audience. This could be based on hobbies, interests, demographics, or product categories.

Product Sourcing: Identify reliable suppliers and brands that align with your subscription box theme. Quality and variety are key factors to consider when selecting products.

Value Proposition: Clearly communicate the value subscribers will receive from your box. Highlight the benefits of the products, customization options, and any exclusive items.

Pricing Strategy: Determine the pricing structure for your subscription plans. Consider factors such as the cost of products, packaging, shipping, and any additional value-added services.

Packaging and Presentation: Design appealing and branded packaging that enhances the unboxing experience. The packaging should align with your subscription box theme and create a sense of excitement.

Subscription Tiers: Offer different subscription tiers with varying levels of products and benefits. This allows customers to choose the option that best suits their preferences and budget.

Customer Engagement: Engage with subscribers through email updates, social media, and community-building activities. Keep them informed about upcoming boxes, product reveals, and promotions.

Quality Control: Ensure the products in your subscription box meet quality standards and accurately represent the theme. Monitor customer feedback and make improvements as needed.

Sustainability: Consider Eco-friendly packaging and sustainable product choices, as these aspects resonate with environmentally conscious consumers.

Marketing Channels: Utilize social media, influence partnerships, and content marketing to promote your subscription box. Engage with potential subscribers through engaging visuals and compelling content.

Feedback and Improvement: Collect feedback from subscribers to continuously improve your subscription box. Adapt to changing preferences and offer a seamless customer experience.

Logistics and Operations: Plan out the logistics of order fulfillment, shipping, and customer support. Choose reliable shipping partners and set clear expectations for delivery times.

Starting a subscription box business requires careful planning, attention to detail, and a deep understanding of your target audience's preferences. By offering unique and valuable products in a convenient and exciting way, you can create a successful and engaging subscription box experience for your customers.

Ten

Home Renovation and Design

Certainly! "Home Renovation and Design" involves offering services that help homeowners transform and improve their living spaces. This business can encompass various aspects, including interior design, renovation project management, and home improvement consulting. Here's a more detailed explanation:

Concept: The home renovation and design business focuses on assisting homeowners in enhancing the aesthetics, functionality, and value of their homes. Whether it's a minor upgrade, a full-scale renovation, or simply a design refresh, this business provides expertise and services to achieve the desired transformation.

Services Offered:

- **Interior Design**: Offering professional design services to create cohesive and aesthetically pleasing interiors that reflect the homeowners' preferences and lifestyles.

- **Home Renovation**: Managing and overseeing renovation projects, coordinating contractors, budgeting, and ensuring timelines are met.
- **Space Planning**: Optimizing the layout and flow of interior spaces to maximize functionality and usability.
- **Color and Material Selection**: Providing guidance on color palettes, materials, finishes, and decor choices that align with the design vision.
- **Consulting Services**: Offering expert advice and recommendations to homeowners who want to make improvements themselves.

Benefits:

- **Enhanced Living Spaces**: Homeowners can achieve spaces that are more comfortable, functional, and visually appealing.
- **Increased Property Value**: Well-executed renovations and design upgrades can increase the resale value of the home.
- **Expertise and Guidance**: Professional designers and project managers bring expertise and knowledge to guide homeowners through the process.
- **Personalization**: Tailored design solutions ensure that the space reflects the homeowners' individual tastes and preferences.

Challenges:

- **Budget Management**: Balancing design aspirations with

budget constraints can be a challenge during renovations.

- **Communication**: Clear communication between homeowners, designers, and contractors is crucial to avoid misunderstandings.
- **Trends and Styles**: Staying updated on design trends and styles to provide contemporary solutions.

Marketing Strategy:

- Showcase Before-and-After Transformations: Highlight the trans-formative power of your services through visual content.
- Portfolio: Create a portfolio showcasing your past projects to demonstrate your expertise.
- Testimonials: Collect and share testimonials from satisfied homeowners.
- Online Presence: Develop a professional website and engage on social media platforms to showcase your work and connect with potential clients.

Technology Considerations: Utilize design software for creating 3D renderings and visualizations, project management tools for tracking progress, and digital communication platforms for efficient client interaction.

Starting a home renovation and design business requires a strong understanding of design principles, project management skills, and effective communication. By helping homeowners bring their design visions to life and create spaces they love, you can make a positive impact on their lives and contribute to the improvement of their living environments

Certainly! Here are some additional aspects to consider when starting a home renovation and design business:

Market Research: Research your local market to understand the demand for home renovation and design services. Identify trends, preferences, and potential competitors.

Target Audience: Define your target audience based on demographics, preferences, and lifestyles. Tailor your services to meet their specific needs.

Licensing and Permits: Depending on your location and the scope of your services, you may need to obtain relevant licenses and permits to operate legally.

Networking: Build relationships with contractors, suppliers, and other professionals in the construction and design industry. Networking can lead to collaborations and referrals.

Project Management: Develop strong project management skills to oversee renovation projects effectively. This includes budgeting, scheduling, and coordinating various contractors.

Contracts and Agreements: Draft clear contracts and agreements that outline the scope of work, timelines, payment terms, and other relevant details. Contracts help prevent misunderstandings.

Safety and Compliance: Ensure that all renovations and design projects adhere to safety regulations and building codes.

Marketing and Branding: Develop a compelling brand identity that reflects your style and expertise. Use a combination of online and offline marketing strategies to reach potential clients.

Portfolio Development: Create a diverse portfolio that showcases a range of projects, styles, and scales. A portfolio helps demonstrate your capabilities to potential clients.

Client Consultation: Offer initial consultations to understand the client's needs, preferences, and budget. This will help you tailor your services to their specific requirements.

Design Software: Familiarize yourself with design software tools that allow you to create visualizations, floor plans, and 3D renderings for client presentations.

Testimonials and Reviews: Collect feedback from satisfied clients and showcase their testimonials on your website and marketing materials. Positive reviews can build credibility.

Continued Learning: Stay updated on design trends, materials, and technologies through workshops, courses, and industry publications.

Sustainability: Consider offering Eco-friendly and sustainable design options that align with growing consumer interest in environmentally conscious solutions.

Starting a home renovation and design business requires a combination of creative flair, project management skills, and strong customer service. By providing personalized design solutions and overseeing renovations with attention to detail, your business can contribute to creating beautiful and functional living spaces for homeowners.

Eleven

Pet Services

Certainly! "Pet Services" encompass a wide range of businesses that cater to the needs of pets and their owners. This industry includes services such as pet grooming, pet sitting, pet training, pet supply retail, and more. Here's a more detailed explanation:

Concept: Pet services involve providing various services and products that enhance the well-being, care, and happiness of pets. These businesses serve as valuable resources for pet owners seeking assistance in caring for their furry friends.

Types of Pet Services:

- **Pet Grooming**: Offering grooming services such as bathing, haircuts, nail trimming, and coat brushing to keep pets clean and well-maintained.
- **Pet Sitting and Boarding**: Providing temporary care for pets when their owners are away, either in the pet owner's

home or at a boarding facility.
- **Pet Training**: Offering training classes and programs to help pets learn obedience commands, behavior modification, and socialization skills.
- **Pet Daycare**: Providing a safe and supervised environment for pets to socialize, play, and receive care during the day.
- **Pet Retail**: Operating pet supply stores that offer a variety of pet products, including food, toys, accessories, and grooming supplies.
- **Pet Photography**: Offering professional photography services to capture memorable moments of pets and their owners.
- **Pet Transportation**: Providing transportation services to help pets travel safely to veterinary appointments, grooming sessions, or other locations.

Benefits:

- **Animal Welfare**: Pet services contribute to the overall health, comfort, and happiness of pets.
- **Convenience for Pet Owners**: These services provide pet owners with support and assistance in meeting their pets' needs.
- **Expertise**: Pet professionals bring specialized knowledge in areas like grooming, training, and health care.
- **Bonding**: Services like training and daycare help pets develop strong bonds with their owners and other pets.

Challenges:

- **Pet Safety**: Ensuring the safety and well-being of pets is a top priority in all aspects of pet services.

- **Customer Trust**: Building trust with pet owners is crucial, as they are entrusting their beloved animals to your care.
- **Regulations**: Depending on your location, there may be regulations and licensing requirements for certain pet services.

Marketing Strategy:

- Promote the expertise of your staff and the quality of care you provide for pets.
- Share before-and-after photos for grooming services to showcase the transformation of pets.
- Use social media to engage with pet owners and share informative content about pet care.

Technology Considerations: Consider using scheduling and appointment management software to streamline bookings, as well as a strong online presence to attract clients.

Starting a pet services business requires a genuine love for animals, a commitment to their well-being, and a focus on delivering high-quality care. By offering services that cater to the needs of pets and their owners, you can create a positive impact on the lives of both furry friends and their human companions.

Certainly! Here are some additional aspects to consider when starting a pet services business:

Pet First Aid and Safety: Gain knowledge of pet first aid and safety procedures to ensure you can respond effectively to any emergencies that may arise.

Client Education: Educate pet owners about the services

you provide, the benefits of proper pet care, and any specific recommendations for their pets' well-being.

Insurance Coverage: Consider obtaining appropriate liability insurance to protect your business from potential risks and incidents involving pets.

Licensing and Regulations: Research local regulations and requirements for operating a pet services business, such as permits and health department inspections.

Cleanliness and Hygiene: Maintain a clean and hygienic environment for pets in your care, whether it's a grooming salon, daycare facility, or boarding service.

Tailored Services: Customize your services to cater to different breeds, sizes, and temperaments of pets. Personalized care enhances the experience for both pets and their owners.

Positive Reinforcement: If offering training services, focus on positive reinforcement methods that reward good behavior and foster a strong bond between pets and owners.

Client Communication: Establish clear communication channels with pet owners, including updates on their pets' well-being and any special instructions.

Business Location: Choose a suitable location for your pet services business, taking into consideration accessibility, visibility, and the local pet owner population.

Pet-Friendly Environment: Ensure that your business environment is safe and welcoming for pets, with appropriate facilities for their comfort and enjoyment.

Staff Training: If you plan to hire staff, provide comprehensive training on pet care, safety protocols, and customer service.

Quality Products: If selling pet products, focus on offering high-quality and safe products that cater to the specific needs of pets.

Community Engagement: Participate in local pet-related events, workshops, and partnerships to build a strong presence within the pet owner community.

Feedback Collection: Regularly collect feedback from pet owners to improve your services and address any concerns.

Niche Focus: Consider specializing in a particular aspect of pet care or a specific pet species (e.g., dog grooming, cat boarding) to differentiate your business.

Starting a pet services business requires a deep understanding of pet behavior, care, and safety. By offering services that prioritize the well-being of pets and providing peace of mind to their owners, you can create a rewarding and impactful business that serves as a valuable resource in your community.

Twelve

Digital Marketing Agency

Certainly! A "Digital Marketing Agency" is a business that provides a range of online marketing services to help clients increase their online visibility, reach their target audience, and achieve their business goals. This industry has grown significantly due to the increasing importance of digital platforms for businesses. Here's a more detailed explanation:

Concept: A digital marketing agency specializes in using various online channels and strategies to promote businesses, products, or services in the digital realm. The agency's primary goal is to help clients build a strong online presence, engage with their target audience, and drive measurable results.

Services Offered:

- **Search Engine Optimization (SEO)**: Optimizing websites to rank higher in search engine results, leading to increased organic (unpaid) website traffic.

- **Pay-Per-Click Advertising (PPC)**: Managing and optimizing paid advertising campaigns on platforms like Google Ads and social media to drive targeted traffic.
- **Social Media Marketing**: Creating and managing social media profiles, posting engaging content, and running paid social media campaigns.
- **Content Marketing**: Developing and distributing valuable and relevant content to attract and engage the target audience.
- **Email Marketing**: Designing and sending email campaigns to nurture leads, engage customers, and drive conversions.
- **Influencer Marketing**: Collaborating with influencers to promote products or services to their audience.
- **Analytics and Reporting**: Analyzing data and providing insights on campaign performance and ROI to clients.

Benefits:

- **Online Visibility**: Digital marketing strategies help businesses become more visible to their target audience in the online space.
- **Audience Engagement**: Engaging content and interactions on digital platforms foster a deeper connection with customers.
- **Measurable Results**: Digital marketing allows for accurate tracking of metrics, enabling clients to assess the effectiveness of campaigns.
- **Scalability**: Digital campaigns can be scaled up or down based on business goals and budget.

Challenges:

- **Constant Changes**: The digital landscape is dynamic, requiring agencies to stay updated on algorithm changes, platform updates, and trends.
- **Competition**: The digital marketing agency market is competitive, so differentiation and expertise are crucial.
- **Client Expectations**: Meeting client expectations and demonstrating tangible results require effective communication and strategy.

Marketing Strategy:

- **Showcase Results**: Highlight successful case studies and before-and-after data to demonstrate the impact of your services.
- **Thought Leadership**: Position your agency as an expert by sharing insightful content on digital marketing trends and strategies.
- **Networking**: Build relationships with potential clients through networking events, industry conferences, and online forums.

Technology Considerations: Utilize digital marketing tools for SEO analysis, social media scheduling, email marketing, and data analytics.

Starting a digital marketing agency requires a solid understanding of digital marketing channels, strategies, and tools. By helping businesses thrive in the digital space, your agency can contribute to their growth and success while navigating the ever-evolving world of online marketing.

Certainly! Here are some additional aspects to consider when starting a digital marketing agency:

Niche Specialization: Consider specializing in a specific industry or niche, such as healthcare, e-commerce, or local businesses. This can help you tailor your services and better understand the unique challenges of that industry.

Target Audience: Define your ideal clients based on factors like industry, company size, and marketing needs. Tailor your services to address their specific pain points.

Skill Set: Build a team with a diverse skill set, including SEO specialists, content creators, social media experts, and data analysts.

Client On-boarding: Develop a process for on-boarding new clients, which includes understanding their goals, conducting an audit of their current digital presence, and proposing a customized strategy.

Transparent Reporting: Provide regular reports that detail the performance of campaigns and the impact on key metrics such as website traffic, conversions, and ROI.

Pricing Structure: Determine your pricing structure based on the services offered, the complexity of campaigns, and the level of involvement required.

Portfolio: Create a portfolio showcasing successful campaigns, client testimonials, and before-and-after results.

Client Relationships: Nurture strong relationships with your clients by maintaining open communication, addressing concerns promptly, and providing proactive recommendations.

Continual Learning: Stay updated on the latest digital marketing trends, algorithm changes, and new tools to ensure your strategies are effective.

Contracts and Agreements: Develop clear contracts and

service agreements that outline scope of work, payment terms, and expectations.

Ethical Practices: Adhere to ethical and best practices in digital marketing, such as respecting user privacy and following platform guidelines.

Networking: Attend industry events, webinars, and conferences to network with potential clients and fellow professionals.

Scaling: Plan for growth by considering how to scale your agency, hire additional staff, and manage an increasing client base.

Branding and Website: Invest in creating a professional website that showcases your services, expertise, and team. Your website is often the first impression for potential clients.

Testimonials and Referrals: Encourage satisfied clients to provide testimonials and refer your services to other businesses.

Cultural Fit: Ensure that your agency's values align with the values of your clients, as a strong cultural fit can lead to more successful collaborations.

Starting a digital marketing agency requires a deep understanding of the digital landscape, strong strategic thinking, and the ability to adapt to changing trends. By helping businesses achieve their online marketing goals, your agency can play a significant role in their growth and success.

Thirteen

Elderly Care and Assistance

Certainly! "Elderly Care and Assistance" involves providing support, companionship, and services to senior individuals who may require help with daily activities, healthcare, and maintaining their overall well-being. This is an essential and rewarding field, especially as the elderly population continues to grow. Here's a more detailed explanation:

Concept: Elderly care and assistance services are designed to improve the quality of life for senior citizens by offering various forms of support. This can range from basic assistance with daily tasks to more specialized healthcare services.

Types of Elderly Care Services:

- **In-Home Care**: Providing assistance with activities of daily living (ADLs) such as bathing, dressing, meal preparation, medication reminders, and housekeeping.

- **Companion Care**: Offering companionship, social interaction, and emotional support to combat feelings of loneliness and isolation.
- **Home Health Care**: Delivering medical services at home, such as wound care, medication management, physical therapy, and monitoring chronic conditions.
- **Assisted Living**: Managing and operating assisted living facilities where seniors can receive both assistance with daily tasks and social engagement.
- **Memory Care**: Providing specialized care for seniors with dementia or Alzheimer's disease, focusing on maintaining their cognitive function and safety.
- **Hospice Care**: Offering end-of-life care and support to individuals with terminal illnesses, ensuring comfort and dignity during their final days.

Benefits:

- **Maintaining Independence**: Elderly care services allow seniors to maintain their independence while receiving the help they need.
- **Quality of Life**: Providing companionship and assistance contributes to the emotional well-being of seniors.
- **Peace of Mind**: Families gain peace of mind knowing that their loved ones are receiving proper care and attention.
- **Preventive Care**: Early detection and intervention can help prevent health issues from escalating.

Challenges:

- **Sensitivity**: Providing care for elderly individuals requires

a high level of sensitivity to their needs and preferences.
- **Healthcare Regulations**: Depending on the level of care provided, there may be regulations and licensing requirements to navigate.
- **Family Dynamics**: Balancing the wishes of the elderly individual with the concerns and preferences of their family can be complex.

Marketing Strategy:

- **Trust and Reputation**: Building a strong reputation for reliability, trustworthiness, and compassionate care is crucial.
- **Online Presence**: Develop a professional website with information about your services, team, testimonials, and contact details.
- **Referrals**: Encourage satisfied clients and their families to provide referrals to potential clients.
- **Community Involvement**: Participate in local senior events, community centers, and healthcare networks to build relationships.

Technology Considerations: Utilize technology to manage schedules, communicate with families, and provide remote monitoring and updates.

Starting an elderly care and assistance business requires a deep sense of empathy, respect for the elderly, and a commitment to providing personalized care. By offering support that enhances the lives of seniors and eases the concerns of their families, your business can make a significant positive impact on aging individuals and their loved ones

Certainly! Here are some additional aspects to consider when starting an elderly care and assistance business:

Client Assessment: Conduct thorough assessments of elderly clients to understand their specific needs, preferences, and level of care required.

Care Plans: Develop personalized care plans for each client based on their individual requirements. These plans outline the services, schedule, and goals of care.

Caregiver Training: Provide comprehensive training to caregivers on topics such as communication, empathy, senior safety, and managing health conditions.

Legal and Regulatory Compliance: Research and understand the legal and regulatory requirements for providing elderly care services in your area.

Licensing and Certification: Depending on the level of care provided, you may need specific licenses and certifications. This can include home health care licenses, first aid certification, and more.

Insurance: Obtain liability insurance to protect your business and clients in case of accidents or incidents.

Client Contracts: Create clear and detailed client contracts that outline the scope of services, payment terms, and expectations.

Communication with Families: Maintain open and transparent communication with the families of elderly clients, providing updates on their well-being and any changes to the care plan.

Client Safety: Implement safety measures to ensure the well-being of clients, such as fall prevention strategies and medication management.

Record Keeping: Maintain accurate and organized records

of client assessments, care plans, and progress reports.

Emergency Plans: Develop protocols for handling emergencies and crises, and train caregivers accordingly.

Cultural Sensitivity: Ensure that your caregivers are culturally sensitive and respectful of the diverse backgrounds of the clients they serve.

Marketing to Families: Tailor your marketing efforts to address the concerns and needs of families seeking care for their elderly loved ones.

Continued Learning: Stay updated on best practices in elderly care, health conditions, and relevant medical advancements.

Feedback and Improvement: Regularly gather feedback from clients and their families to improve your services and address any concerns.

Wellness Programs: Consider offering wellness programs that promote physical, mental, and emotional well-being for seniors.

Transportation Services: If feasible, offer transportation services to help seniors get to appointments, run errands, and participate in social activities.

Community Outreach: Collaborate with local senior centers, healthcare providers, and organizations to establish your presence and build trust.

Starting an elderly care and assistance business requires a deep commitment to the well-being of seniors and a genuine desire to provide compassionate care. By offering services that enhance the quality of life for the elderly population, you can make a meaningful difference in their lives and provide invaluable support to their families

Fourteen

Conclusion

Certainly! "Elderly Care and Assistance" involves providing various services to senior individuals to enhance their well-being, independence, and quality of life. This field encompasses in-home care, medical services, companionship, and more. Here's a summary of key points:

Concept: Elderly care services offer support and assistance to seniors who may require help with daily tasks, healthcare, and emotional well-being.

Services Offered: In-home care, companion care, home health care, assisted living, memory care, and hospice care.

Benefits: Maintains independence, improves quality of life, offers emotional support, and provides peace of mind to families.

Challenges: Requires sensitivity, compliance with regulations, balancing family dynamics, and addressing specific health needs.

Marketing Strategy: Focus on building trust, establishing an online presence, leveraging referrals, and engaging with the community.

Technology: Use technology for scheduling, communication, monitoring, and providing updates to families.

Considerations: Client assessments, personalized care plans, caregiver training, legal compliance, insurance, transparent communication with families, safety measures, and record-keeping.

Impact: By offering compassionate care and support, businesses in this field contribute to the well-being and happiness of elderly individuals and their families.

Starting an elderly care and assistance business requires empathy, professionalism, and a commitment to personalized care. It involves understanding the unique needs of seniors and providing services that enhance their lives in meaningful ways